F. Ernest Jackson
and his School

Figure 1

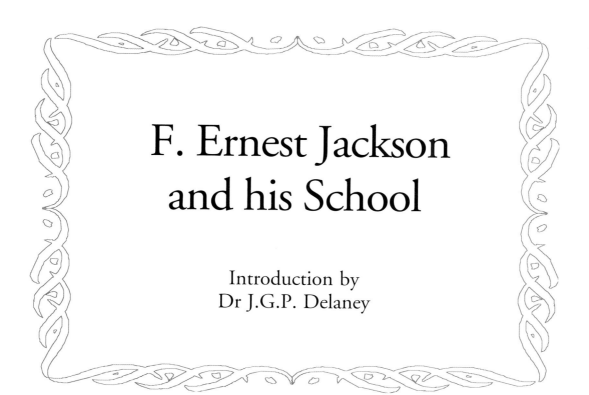

F. Ernest Jackson
and his School

Introduction by
Dr J.G.P. Delaney

ASHMOLEAN MUSEUM
OXFORD
— 2000 —

In Memory of George Warner Allen (1916–1988)

Published to coincide with an exhibition at the Ashmolean Museum,
Oxford 21 March – 4 June 2000

Cover illustration: *The Black Hat*, lithograph (cat. no. 7)

ISBN 1 85444 134 5
British Library Catalogue-in-Publication data:
A catalogue record of this book is available from the British Library
Designed by Andrew Ivett
Typeset in Garamond
Printed in England by Grillford Ltd, Milton Keynes MK1 1QZ, 2000

Foreword

The Ashmolean is deeply grateful for the unstinting help which it has received from many people during the organisation of this exhibition. Dr J.G.P. Delaney who wrote the eloquent introduction has been a much valued adviser and a major lender and has capped his generosity by giving a choice group of drawings by George Warner Allen and Brian Thomas to the museum. Charles Stewart, equally, has been a constant source of encouragement and help and has given to the museum a most welcome collection of drawings by F.E. Jackson. The assistance of the artist's daughter, Mrs Betty Clark, has been indispensable and has been given with unfailing kindness at all times. John and Helen Standen have been no less generous. We are particularly grateful to them for making an essential contribution towards the cost of conserving two paintings by Jackson, belonging to the Ashmolean, which has enabled us to include them in the exhibition. We are also most grateful to Mrs Mary Edmonds, Mr and Mrs Lea Wilson, Mr Nicholas Savage and Thelma Winyard, archivist of the Byam Shaw School, for help at various stages and to the many lenders who have asked to remain anonymous. Most of the photography has been undertaken with customary efficiency and good-will by Mrs Jane Inskipp in the museum photographic studio, assisted by Mrs Cath Casley, and the large task of conserving the works on paper in time for the exhibition has been carried out with equal care and efficiency by Miss Alice Powell. Our thanks, too, to Miss Katie Heard and Miss Geraldine Glynn for administering the loans and to Mr Robert Johnson whose expertise in hanging exhibitions has been indispensable as ever.

Christopher Brown
Director, Ashmolean Museum

F.E. Jackson and his School
by Dr J.G.P. Delaney

Few artists have been remembered with such loyalty by his admirers, and yet so forgotten by art historians, as Ernest Jackson (fig. 1). A dwindling number of students, who admire him as a man and an artist as well as a teacher, still speak of him with reverence. Yet to the art-loving public he is unknown, except for a few warm references in the autobiographies of fellow artists such as A.S. Hartrick and C.R.W. Nevinson. The qualities which so impressed his contemporaries were substantial ones and deserve wider recognition. It is time that his work and his key role in the art world of his day were better known.

Jackson's lack of fame is partly due to his total devotion to his art and to his unwillingness to publicize himself. "I want to live in obscurity" he would say. "Remember, you can't do things *and* get the credit for them. Getting the credit is a wholetime job" [1]. Even in his own day, he was not a household name, but he was well known to the cognoscenti for his artistic gifts as well as for his wide scholarship and cultivated mind.

Jackson's drawings were particularly admired. Augustus John described him as "a very fine draughtsman – indeed one of the best not only of his period, but of the whole of British art" [2]. Sir Gerald Kelly, P.R.A., recalled that during nearly twenty years when Jackson taught at the Royal Academy Schools, "many of his pupils regarded him as one of the greatest draughtsmen England ever had, and how right they were" [3]. His contribution to lithography, the other field in which he was pre-eminent, was also recognized. "Lithography in England today" said the distinguished lithographer, John Copley, "is really his creation" [4]. That the enthusiasm of his contemporaries should have been so soon forgotten would not have surprised Jackson, but he would probably have affirmed that good work would eventually find its rightful place. And so it will.

Francis Ernest Jackson was a Yorkshireman, born in Lockwood, Huddersfield, on 15 August 1872. He was generally a courteous man, but he could also have that gruff and forthright manner which is said to typify his fellow Yorkshiremen. After his parents moved to Leeds, he was apprenticed as a lithographer to a local firm of printers, Messrs. Knight & Foster, perhaps because his father was a stationer. His keenness attracted the attention of the head of the firm, Mr Knight,

1. Recorded by Brian Thomas in "Reminiscences of Jackson", Jackson Papers, Tate Gallery Archives. This collection (hereafter "Ovens") was gathered and preserved by Pamela Ovens, I wish to thank the many people who have discussed Jackson with me or corresponded with me about him, especially his daughter, Mrs Betty Clark and the late George Warner Allen, the late Pamela Ovens, Charles Stewart, the late Brian Dick Thomas, the late Peter Greenham, the late Dorothy Hutton, the late Max Chapman, the late Richard Finny, and Jane Greenham. I would also like to thank the Faculté des études supérieures et de la recherche de l'Université de Moncton for a travel grant while I was preparing this introduction.
2. Augustus John to Pamela Ovens, 22 Nov 1955 (Ovens).
3. Sir Gerald Kelly to Pamela Ovens, quoted in *Ernest Jackson Drawings and Lithographs* [1955].
4. John Copley to Brian Thomas, quoted in *The Burlington Magazine*, 88 (Nov 1946), p. 280.

who not only encouraged him, but also allowed him to draw in his garden where he acquired his life-long love of depicting flowers [5]. At Yorkshire College (now Leeds University), he is said to have joined, possibly as an evening student, the life-class under Frank Suddards, who taught textile design as well as drawing [6]. It was probably he who encouraged Jackson to go to Paris, then the Mecca of art students, where he spent two years. With the assistance of Mr Knight and an uncle, he went to the Atelier Julian in 1895, the foremost of the independent teaching studios, where he studied under Bouguereau, and then on to the more conservative Ecole des Beaux-Arts. He also received lessons from Jean-Paul Laurens, Gabriel Ferrier and Benjamin-Constant. At this time his chief love was decorative painting and his heroes were Giotto, Tintoretto and Rubens. He recalled how "liberally one pounded with adverse criticism the paintings one saw in the exhibitions of that time which were not fortunate enough to conform to those exalted standards of excellence which one set on high for all & either to attain and be worshipped or fail to reach & be eternally damned". However, the wise words of one of his teachers struck him and remained with him for life: "In art you cannot do what you would ...do; you must do that which you can do" [7]. At Julian's, despite his very English appearance and character, he had been "one of the only English students who could pass as a Frenchman" [8]. He learned to speak excellent French, met Degas and Monet (stories of whom he later told his students) and spent three months, one summer, boating and painting on the Seine. During these "happy and irresponsible" days, he supported himself by doing textile designs which he would return to sell in England periodically.

By 1900, he had settled in London, in Glebe Place, which was then cheap, unfashionable and a haunt of artists. He became one of a group of young artists who dubbed themselves "the Depressionists" and who spent too much time and money at the Café Royal [9]. At first, he devoted himself to poster design and to a series of decorative watercolours in the Art Nouveau style. His work was immediately noticed and in 1900 four examples "so interesting both in treatment and in refinement" were reproduced in *The Studio* [10].

While Jackson was in France, he had developed an interest in artistic lithography. The technique of printing by lithography, discovered by Senefelder at the end of the eighteenth century, had been perfected by French artists in the first half of the nineteenth century but it had then declined as an art form until revived by the Impressionists and their colleagues. Jackson admired the lithographs of French artists from this second flourishing of the art – Forain, Steinlen, Toulouse-Lautrec and others – and kept examples of their work all his life. Back in London, he enrolled as a student at the School of Photo-Engraving and Lithography in Bolt Court under Mr Baxter, the leading teacher of trade lithography of the day [11]. Trade lithography was a reproductive technique, used largely for reproducing photographic illustrations in magazines and

5. F.L.Jackson, the artist's brother, to Pamela Ovens, 15 Aug 1949; letter to Pamela Ovens, dated Salisbury 23 Feb [1946] in which the last page and signature are missing (Ovens).
6. J. Roach, Registrar of the University of Leeds, to Pamela Ovens, 11 Sep 1952 (Ovens).
7. "Untitled Lecture", undated manuscript [1940s] (Ovens).
8. Brian Thomas, *The Burlington Magazine*, 88 (Nov 1946),p. 279.
9. Orlando Ward to Pamela Ovens, 23 Sep 1949 (Ovens).
10. "Studio Talk", *The Studio*, 18 (1900), p. 281.
11. Sidney Tushingham to Pamela Ovens, 14 Sep 1949 (Ovens).

sometimes for reproducing the works of artists. A highly skilled trade lithographer copied the design onto stone and it was then printed by an equally skilled printer. Trade lithographers were very secretive about the process and charged dearly for their work. Artists generally regarded lithography as a difficult and expensive medium and avoided it.

Jackson made a fundamental contribution to changing the situation of lithography in Britain. Having learned the skills of the trade, he was able to teach his fellow artists how to print their own work and dispense with the professionals. Using chalks and inks composed of soap and tallow, the artist would draw directly onto a smooth stone slab. The stone was then moistened by a damp cloth. The greasy design repelled the wet while the untouched parts of the stone absorbed the moisture. When lithographic ink was applied with a roller, it adhered to the design but not to the moistened parts of the surface. A sheet of damp paper was then placed on the stone and passed through a press to obtain an impression. Sometimes a drawing was done first on paper and transferred to the stone, a method later used by Whistler. Jackson, however, felt that the effects of transfer lithography were inferior to those where the design was drawn directly onto the stone [12]. In either case, the result was an original print that faithfully reproduced the artist's drawing.

Although Whistler, Charles Shannon, Alphonse Legros and William Rothenstein had produced artistic lithographs in England, few others took it up until Jackson's classes made the process widely accessible. Not only did he open the first studio in London to teach original lithography but he remained the chief teacher for twenty years. In the 1890s, Shannon published several lithographs in *The Dial*, the periodical he produced with his friend, Charles Ricketts, but, according to A.S. Hartrick: "the real effort to introduce lithography to artists did not come until F.E. Jackson returned from Paris and began to teach the whole craft of lithography in classes of the L.C.C. Art Schools". Hartrick pointed out that Jackson "supplied the opportunity to learn all that was to be known about drawing on stone and about printing from it" [13]. As he taught at several art schools, his influence was widespread: Croydon (until 1908), Camberwell (1903–13), Chelsea (1905–22) and, most importantly, the Central School of Arts and Crafts (1902–21), where he also gave classes in life drawing. Consequently, many lithographers of the succeeding generation, were taught by him.

Jackson felt that a lithographer should be master of all aspects of his art and should print his own work. For this reason he maintained that Shannon, rather than Whistler, had been the real reviver of artistic lithography in England [14]. Shannon had printed all his own work whereas, as Jackson pointed out, Whistler had the good fortune to have had the assistance of a very able lithographer called Bray, "that delicate and sensitive artist with the lithographic printing roller" [15]. Had Whistler learned to use a printing press himself, however, Jackson felt that he would have been able to produce lithographs "far surpassing in beauty any that came from his hand". Indeed, he believed that the process itself of printing a colour print could contribute to the final effect.

---

12. *Print Collector's Quarterly*, 11 (1925), p. 214.
13. Hartrick, *Painter's Pilgrimage*, p. 217
14. Jackson, "Lecture on Lithography", manuscript (Ovens).
15. *Print Collector's Quarterly* 11 (1925), p. 214.

After printing each colour the effect "should be considered and other colours added as they appear necessary to the final printing". In this way, "the printer is used as a designing medium" like a palette knife, and since the roller could be manipulated to produce much variety of effect, the artist was thus capable of producing a print "which has quite a character of its own and does not resemble a work in any other medium" [16].

Along with teaching the technical side of printing, Jackson also gave his students a sense of the higher values of printmaking. "You should know" he continued "that accident & little touches of colour do not make a print. More final & considered design are required ... the whole philosophy of a print lies in this – the accidental eliminated, the final, ie., the permanent & unchangeable recorded in a noble design. Amen" [17].

Jackson began working in lithography as soon as he returned from France. As early as 1898, he designed two large posters (60 x 40 ins) for Robbs Biscuits. These were not lithographed by himself but were transferred to the stone by his friend, R.G. Praill, and printed at the Avenue Press. One of them depicted children sitting on the ground playing with soldiers [18]. It was not long, however, before Jackson was printing his own designs. He made his mark immediately. In 1904, his lithographs were featured in an article in *The Studio*. Some of the works illustrated were genre pieces, like *The Buccaneer* (cat. 6), a lithograph for which Jackson had a particular fondness and which he exhibited frequently, and *Chicot the Jester*. These were studies from models that showed "proof of unmistakable talent for character-seizing". This skill served Jackson well in doing lithographic portraits, one of his principal sources of income outside his teaching. A study of roses in a Chinese vase was praised as a "true lithographer's drawing". It was "not one that could have been done upon paper" [19]. Jackson also did a series of delicate, monochrome lithographs of carnations, of tulips, of camelias and five of roses (eg. cat. 11). These are wonderful examples of the use of texture in lithography.

The two lithographs that Jackson exhibited at the Paris Salon in 1909 earned him an honorable mention. One of these was *The Buccaneer*. The other, entitled *The Black Hat* (cat. 7), was a portrait of his future wife, Gertrude Templeton, whom he married in 1910. She was the subject of some of his best works of this period. *La Robe de Velours* (cat. 9), one of several portraits of Mrs Jackson, uses the breadth of tone and texture that is characteristic of the medium to suggest the varying qualities of skin, hair and velvet. Here, too, is an indication of the splendid rich blacks obtainable in lithography. In contrast, the background is sketched in with a lighter hand. At the Paris Salon of 1911, *La Robe de Velours* was exhibited along with a portrait of his wife, *Effet de Lumière*, of c.1909 (cat. 10). These were singled out as "two of the most beautiful portraits of the year" in the *Gazette de Beaux-Arts* which included an original print of the *Effet de Lumière* in the same issue [20]. An impression of this was bought for the French national collection.

---

16. Jackson, "Lecture on Lithography", manuscript (Ovens)
17. "Extract from a letter of 1914 about a print", transcript (Ovens).
18. R.G.Praill to Byam Shaw School, 16 and 20 Nov 1946 (Ovens).
19. Ernest Radford, *The Studio* (1904), p. 137.
20. *Gazette des Beaux-Arts*, 6 (1911), p. 47

Figure 2

Jackson also did a few etchings in this period. One of the most beautiful, entitled *The Profile* (cat. 8), is another portrait of his wife, sitting, holding a finely bound book in her lap. Some of the props, including the ginger jar on the shelf, reappear in *La Robe de Velours*. Among his other etchings are two views drawn in France, *L'Eglise de Varsay* and *L'allée des Marmoutiers, Versailles* (cat. 33). These were exhibited at the International Society in London in 1911 along with an etched portrait. Jackson then seems to have abandoned etching. One might have expected that the linear qualities of the etching needle would have appealed to a draughtsman who had a genius for line and who manipulated the pen, on occasion, with an etcher's precision. However, he evidently preferred the greater variety of tone and texture available through lithographic chalk and wash which left him ample scope to exercise his skill in drawing.

Portraiture forms the bulk of Jackson's lithographs. For a lithographic portrait, he charged twenty guineas. Though some of these are of more general interest than others, they always show great skill and subtlety. Many were commissions from friends and patrons. His reputation in this branch of his art led to his inclusion among a number of artists commissioned by *The Daily Chronicle* to commemorate the coronation of King George V in 1911 in a set of lithographs. These were first published from zinc blocks in the newspaper and issued afterwards in a memorial portfolio. Jackson contributed a portrait of Mary, the new queen, which was published on 16 June 1911.

In 1921, Jackson's lithograph of Henry Festing Jones (1851–1928), the friend and biographer of Samuel Butler, was reproduced in *Vogue* (cat. 30). Comparison with the preparatory drawing (cat. 29) shows how the artist adapted it to his medium by, for instance, darkening the background to bring out the delicate and masterly drawing of the face. Jackson also received a number of private commissions for portraits in this period, including two from the artist, Mary Sargant Florence, who asked him to draw her children, Philip (cat. 15) and Alix (cat. 14). The more interesting of the two is the one of Philip (exhibited 1912) who is depicted looking out the window and wearing his jacket from Caius College, Cambridge. The portrait of Alix, who entered the Bloomsbury set when she married James Strachey and is shown as a rather earnest, modern young woman with cropped hair, must be contemporary. In 1909, on Mary Sargant Florence's recommendation, Jackson had portrayed her sister, the distinguished biologist, Miss Ethel Sargant, sitting at a work table (fig. 2). He included her microscope in the picture but she complained that her "sense of humour was left out" [21]. Despite this, she bought thirteen extra copies for nine guineas. Through her, Jackson did portraits of a Mrs Don and her son, David (cat. 16), who was

21. Ethel Sargant to F.E.Jackson, 8 Jan 1910 (Ovens).

a naval cadet at Osborne. This commissioned portrait, like that of Philip Sargant Florence, is one of the few that Jackson chose to exhibit widely.

Like Whistler, Jackson also did some architectural subjects. A number of these, including his views of St Riquier (cat. 22; exhibited 1913), the Château d'Amboise (exhibited 1915) and the Pont Neuf, Paris (exhibited 1922), were drawn in France. The first was issued in a special edition for the lay-members (non-artists) of the Senefelder Club, an association founded by Jackson and his colleagues to promote lithography. A few portraits were also done in France, including a lithographic portrait of a young French girl (cat. 26), drawn during the First World War when he was at Rouen [22]. This may have been *The Refugee*, exhibited in 1919 at the Senefelder Club. After the war, most summer holidays were spent travelling in France. On these occasions, he did hundreds of drawings and watercolours of Paris streets, of French churches (cat. 22 and 36) and of the countryside. The fountains of Versailles had a special fascination for him (cats 30–31) and, in addition to the etching, were the subject of several watercolours. His love of France was repaid

Figure 3

since his work was honoured there before it received wide recognition in England. After the honourable mention of his lithographs in 1909, he won a silver medal at the Salon of 1929 and his work became *hors concours* at the annual exhibitions.

Among the most original and personal of his lithographs were those of his own homes. *Evening Snow in London* of 1910/11 (cat. 12 and 13) may represent a view in the neighbourhood of his home in Phillimore Gardens in Kensington where he lived before his marriage, seen through snow. This was inspired, perhaps, by Charles Shannon's print of his own house, *The Vale in Snow,* of 1899. *Evening Snow* was printed at the Chelsea Polytechnic lithography class where a copy was given to each student [23]. Jackson tried many effects with this atmospheric lithograph which exists in at least four states, printed in black, blue, black on blue and in beige on blue. Three prints depict Morton House, Chiswick Mall, where he lived from 1912 until 1919 when he moved to Mall Cottage, a smaller house nearby. *The Door* (fig. 3), exhibited in 1913, gives us a glimpse through the entrance of the house, with its Georgian fanlight, over the gardens to the river. While the floors, wall, curtain and shadows are in wash, the rest is done mainly in chalk, producing a wide variety of effects. Only fifty copies of this print were made, the usual maximum

22. Margaret James to Pamela Ovens, 25 Aug 1949 (Ovens)
23. Elsie de Coudenhove (née Henderson) to Pamela Ovens, 6 Nov 1949 (Ovens).

which he allowed for an edition of his work. Morton House was also the site of *The Back Door* (exhibited 1913) and *The Garden* (cat. 20; exhibited 1915).

In 1918, the London County Council embarked on a plan for a series of lithographs to be hung in schools in the hope of improving artistic taste. Jackson was made technical adviser to the scheme and contributed a large coloured lithograph (cat. 25) of *Lambeth Palace* (1918/19) where the stylization of the river shows some vestige of his earlier Art Nouveau manner. Proposing subjects illustrating "THE LAND, ARCHITECTURE, the work of man on the land, and HISTORICAL EVENTS & PORTRAITS", Jackson stated that the ideal school picture should be "diagrammatic and detailed" in design; "it should be finely drawn & beautiful in colour & its 'treatment' should be such as would make for visibility in class teaching". Finally, he felt that "there should be an explanatory inscription in legible lettering which should be designed in conjunction with the pictorial side of the work" [24]. Though he had high hopes for this project and foresaw international exchanges, it collapsed after the publication of a few prints.

Like the large print of Lambeth Palace, some of Jackson's most accomplished lithographs are those in colour. *Sweet Williams* (cat. 28) is printed in a rich harmony of colours in several different combinations. In one of these, the vase is printed in blue, brown and yellow while the flowers are purple, blue, mauve. pink and grey and the leaves are dark green. The background is gold and yellow. Another version has a red background, flecked with real gold leaf. Some of the colour effects are achieved by overprinting two primary colours, a technique that requires great dexterity in such a small print, a mere 6 $7/8$ x 6 $1/2$ inches. A portrait that Jackson regarded as one of his best was a wash lithograph of the print-maker, Elsie Henderson, one of his pupils at the Chelsea Polytechnic [25]. *The Release* (cat. 27), printed in pale colours, has a sinuous linearity which is reminiscent of the Art Nouveau style that had influenced his earlier work. The inscription on the print "Ernest Jackson del et imp" (Ernest Jackson drew and printed this) is commonly found on original prints but it had a special significance for Jackson who did more than anyone in England in the early 1900s to combine the work of the artist with the craft of lithographic printing.

Jackson took a leading role as a propagandist for his art. In 1907, along with three colleagues, he founded *The Neolith*, a quarterly magazine printed entirely in lithography. Though only four numbers were published over two years, it printed contributions, including three by Jackson, by all the leading lithographers of the day and stirred new interest in the medium, especially among artists working in black and white. Another magazine, *The Imprint*, which Jackson helped to found in 1913, was devoted to improving standards of typography and printing methods, including lithography on which he wrote a series of articles. Nine monthly issues were printed before it folded. However, he made his greatest contribution to the promotion of lithography in 1910 when, along with A. S. Hartrick, J. Kerr-Lawson and, later, Joseph Pennell, he founded the Senefelder Club. The founders purchased a second-hand press and rented a studio in Chelsea where members could print their work for a small fee. Later they arranged with a commercial printer to use his facilities to produce their own works. Many of the early members, including

---

24. Jackson to unknown correspondent, Morton House, Chiswick, 22 Jan 1917 (Ovens). .
25. Jackson to Mr Longden, 15 Oct 1935 (Ovens).

Elsie Henderson, Ethel Gabain, Lily Blatherwick and Dorothy Hutton, had been trained by Jackson. He also gave two or three lessons to Augustus John who was a member [26]. Most, although not all of the leading British lithographers of the day belonged to the club. The foreign members included Steinlen, Forain and Matisse. By its exhibitions at home and abroad, it did more than anything else to make lithography popular among artists and collectors. Most of Jackson's hundred or so lithographs were shown here from 1910 to 1930.

Because of Jackson's involvement with the Senefelder Club, Frank Pick, head of the London Electric Railway, as the Underground was then called, approached Jackson in an attempt to improve poster design, encourage good artists to work for the company and raise the standard of printing. Jackson asked eight members of the Senefelder Club to design posters in black and white that would encourage people to travel by the underground. Places of beauty or interest were to be depicted in a standard size of 30 x 20 inches. A first group of posters developed the theme of the railway in connection with the Thames. Joseph Pennell showed the river at Charing Cross and Frank Brangwyn illustrated a scene of shipping at Wapping. Jackson's contribution was a large monochrome lithograph (cat. 21) entitled *Chiswick Mall at Stamford Brook* (1913), a view looking down the street where he lived. The series was a great success, both commercially and artistically, and was soon bought by collectors. A signed set of proofs was presented to the Victoria and Albert Museum in 1914. Not long after they had first appeared, Jackson, noticing a crowd outside St James's underground station, asked a policeman if there had been an accident. "No", he was told, "It's some pictures or other" [27]. This venture led to the commission of a long series of distinguished posters by London Transport, including three more done by Jackson.

In 1917, Pick had the idea of commissioning more posters for use in huts, messes and dug-outs by the troops in France. He turned, again, to Jackson who supervised four lithographs designed by Charles Sims, Walter West, George Clausen and himself. Jackson's poster illustrated Thomas Campbell's poem, *Song to the Evening Star*. At the same time, he was technical adviser to the Ministry of Information's *Britain's Efforts and Ideals* series. Eighteen leading artists were asked to contribute twelve "Ideals" in colour and six "Efforts" in black and white. While some, like Shannon, Augustus John and Frank Brangwyn had experience of lithography, others, like Muirhead Bone, Greiffenhagen and Clausen had never done a lithograph in colour. In addition to his own colour print, *Defence against Aggression: England and France* (cat. 24), Jackson approached the artists, supplied them with materials, advised and instructed those new to the art, provided proofs for the artists' inspection, supervised the printing and, finally, organized a ten-shilling contribution from each artist as a tip for the printers. The extent to which the artists appreciated his role was summed up by Gerard Moira on handing over his design: "I leave it in the hands of God and Ernest Jackson" [28]. According to Brian Thomas, the British Government

---

26. P. Greenham to the author; but John himself implies this in his tribute to Jackson printed in *Ernest Jackson Drawings and Lithographs*.
27. Recorded by Pamela Ovens (Ovens).
28. Gerald Moira to Jackson, 14 May 1917 (Ovens).

offered him a decoration for his work but, instead, he "officially requested – and was granted – a holiday in Paris at Government expense!" [29].

In 1921, a change occurred in Jackson's career which turned him away from lithography. Charles Sims, Keeper of the Royal Academy Schools, invited him to become professor of drawing at the RA Schools on the strength of some drawings exhibited by Jackson at the New English Art Club. His superb draughtsmanship had always counted in his lithographs. He was unsurpassed among his contemporaries in teaching artists to understand the construction of the human form and was widely regarded as the successor to Tonks, the leading teacher of the preceding generation. He taught by demonstration which he considered the only method of teaching art and every mark he made on the student's sheet was accompanied by an explanation of its function. Bernard Dunstan recalled Jackson as a "florid and rather formidable figure" but a "charismatic teacher". Jackson "would tap a student on the shoulder, hold out his hand for his, or her, pencil, and proceed, with a minimum of talk, to demonstrate certain essential movements or relationships of form on a corner of a student's paper". Such demonstrations could "develop into complete and beautiful statements, or explorations, of the subtleties of the model's pose as Jackson became engrossed in his work" or be no more than "a clarifying diagram" [30]. The ten or fifteen such drawings that might be done in a teaching day were treasured by the students who sometimes sold or exchanged them. Thus, hundreds of Jackson's demonstration drawings and oil sketches, made for the students in the drawing and painting classes, still survive.

Drawing, Jackson insisted, was not an imitation of nature, an illusion of outside appearances, nor a representation of the outlines of things, but an intellectual exercise, an interpretation of nature. "In figurative drawing" he said in one of his lectures, "the intention of the artist is to make a kind of explanatory diagram of the object drawn" [31]. Elsewhere, he wrote that the object of drawing "was to give the sense of solid form by means of line". Line did the work in a drawing: shading assisted it. He would encourage his students to "feel round" the form as if they were insects crawling round round its contours [32].

Surprisingly, Jackson maintained that he had learned nothing from his own masters. According to Peter Greenham "he used to say that, after leaving the Ecole des Beaux-Arts, he discovered a disastrous difference between his own drawings and the drawings which he loved of the Old Masters. He began to make copies of Raphael, Rubens, Watteau, Holbein and Leonardo, until it flashed upon him that these drawings were not always elegant, not always finished, not always gracious, but always legible: it was a favourite word of his to describe the quality in good drawings most to be desired. They could be read. Looking at them an artist could see which way all the surface of the form went" [33]. It was particularly from studying the drawings of Holbein, which he found in the Louvre, and of Raphael, whom he preferred to Michelangelo, that he derived his lucid style of drawing.

29. Brian Thomas, *The Burlington Magazine*, 88 (Nov 1946), p. 279.
30. B. Dunstan, *The Paintings of Bernard Dunstan* (1993), pp. 9-10.
31. "Lecture on Drawing", manuscript (Ovens).
32. L. Glasson, *Notes from the Sketchbook of F. Ernest Jackson*, 1947, p. 7.
33. P. Greenham, "F. E. Jackson", typescript (Ovens).

Teaching seems to have run in Jackson's family. His grandfather, an uncle, a brother and a sister were all school teachers. Jackson enjoyed encouraging and guiding young people along the road to becoming artists and inspired them with a sense of the nobility of their calling. "I always think" he wrote to one of his students, "that we are so much richer than those who do not paint or draw" [34]. With any sincere struggle or slow development in a student, he showed the greatest patience, but he was always the master and knew how to put the students in their place. When the young George Warner Allen, looking at a drawing by the great French draughtsman, Ingres, confessed: "Oh Sir, I do not think it's very good, but I suppose I've got bad taste", Jackson retorted: "Allen, you've got no taste at all. That is why you have come to me". Nor did he tolerate pretentiousness even in important figures in the art world. At a dinner for the collector, Sir Herbert Cook, he was told by Sir Alec Martin, chairman of Christie's, about a disagreement which Martin had with Tonks over a drawing by Watteau. "I reckon I know as much about Watteau as Tonks", Martin asserted. "Really", Jackson replied, "then would you mind just making me a drawing of an ear" [35].

However, when he conversed more informally with his students during breaks or after lessons, there was usually a benign smile on his lips or a twinkle in his eye as he told them amusing stories of the Old Masters. Taking down a book of reproductions of the work of artists whom he loved, he would comment: "Beautiful things, don't you know". He used to say that a friend had told him that his voice changed when he spoke of Rembrandt, perhaps the artist whom he admired more than any other, although, as with Holbein, he preferred his drawings to his paintings. "I think both men said quite effectively all they had to say in those superb drawings" [36]. Teasing and sparring with his pupils, he usually got the last word. "You can't beat nature, can you?" one new student observed. "No" replied Jackson, "but she can certainly beat you". "*Courage*", he would often say in French to those who faltered, "don't try to be perfect, try and improve".

Not only a superb teacher of technique, Jackson also instilled into his students a humanistic attitude to art. Nothing in life was lost to artists, he told them: living, suffering, overcoming difficulties were all of value to them and would make their work deeper and better. Drawing, moreover, was an excellent training for the mind. "No pursuit other than drawing that I know", he wrote, "will develop the faculties of observation and concentration so fully, and I would go further and assert that constant study of the human form is the best of all means to the cultivation of fine taste in the visual arts". He believed, for instance, that "constant development by means of drawing was the key to the development of Leonardo's marvellous mind" [37]. The qualities developed by drawing were applicable to all aspects of life, so that an artist was capable of handling everyday matters efficiently, better than politicians or businessmen, but he would warn his students: "don't let them know you can do it or you will never get any peace" [38]. Jackson's own reliable character and organizational skills led to his being asked to join many committees in the art world, several of which he headed.

34. Margaret Vaughan to Pamela Ovens, nd (Ovens).
35. Recorded by Brian Thomas, George Warner Allen and others.
36. "Untitled Lecture", manuscript [1940s] (Ovens).
37. "Lecture on Drawing", manuscript (Ovens).
38. Recorded by Margaret Ovey (Ovens).

Yet, while teaching his method of drawing and painting, Jackson did not try to impose his character or his preferences in art on his students. "It was his special gift", Peter Greenham recalled, "to let you be yourself, never to try and make you what you were not. 'Everyone is different' he used to say, 'so you are sure to be original'. Of all our opinions, the only one which ever vexed him were those in which an artist was run down for not being someone else". Greenham once heard Jackson reproach a student who had disparaged Hals in favour of his beloved Rembrandt: "He was different from Rembrandt; he was Hals" [39].

Figure 4

In the 1920s, when teaching drawing made him turn more to drawing for its own sake, he did a series of figure drawings for Colnaghi's (fig. 4). Cats, which he loved, provided him with a more informal source of models. He often uses the cat's markings to model the form and captures the animal's soft, furry quality with a delicate chalk or pencil (cat. 46). Since his cat drawings have often hung in the Friends' Room in the Royal Academy and three from the Academy's collection have been made into best-selling post-cards, these engaging, private studies have now become Jackson's best known works.

Jackson's interest in the technical side of art led him to experiment with different media, tempera, distemper and true fresco, and to master these techniques. In 1901, just after his return to London from Paris, a group of artists formed the Society of Painters in Tempera with the aim of reviving interest in the techniques of the early masters. The technique of tempera painting, in particular, was very imperfectly understood at this date. Even Ruskin did not realize that the early Italian artists had painted in tempera, rather than in oil which had replaced the older medium by the early sixteenth century. He was astonished when he came upon Christiana Herringham making a copy in tempera of a painting in the National Gallery. It was her annotated translation of the late fourteenth-century *Book of the Art of Cennino Cennini,* the most important ancient source for information on early tempera painting, published in 1899, that had made these techniques available to artists and led to the foundation of the Tempera Society. Jackson was not one of the founder members and was not represented in the first exhibition in 1905. However, he had joined the society by the time of the second exhibition at the Baillie Gallery in 1909 at which he exhibited a work in fresco.

From working and discussing with fellow members like James Kerr-Lawson and Mrs Mary Sargant Florence, Jackson learned the requisite skills in tempera painting. The medium of tempera is based on egg, using the yolk, the white or the whole egg, and coloured powders, to which is added water and, sometimes, an oil such as spike of lavender (which smells wonderful). The use

39. P. Greenham, "F.E. Jackson", typescript (Ovens).

of tempera requires the artist to prepare his own pigments and apply the paint in small, precise strokes as it dries quickly. Because of the egg yolk, each batch only lasts for a couple of days. Later, Jackson would often expatiate to his students on the superiority of tempera to oil. Although some artists felt that tempera painting should be pale like fresco, he believed that tempera colour should be rich. His own work in this medium is notable for its jewel-like colours. His early portrait of his daughter, Betty (cat. 39), and the profile portrait of Penryn Monk (cat. 40) show not only his clarity of colour but his debt to the formal qualities of Renaissance art [40]. Dorothy Hutton, who was a close associate, was the model for his tempera painting, *The Manuscript* (cat. 43), and posed for a number of contemporary portraits (eg. cat. 45). Jackson also did at least one flower painting, *Marigolds*, in this medium.

In 1922, Jackson became secretary of the Tempera Society. At the large exhibition held by the society in Brighton that year he exhibited a portrait and *Marigolds* and gave a lecture on the history of the society and on the techniques of tempera and fresco painting. In addition to painting a Pietà in distemper, a medium based on size or glue, he also completed a painting of Eve and some decorations in true fresco. The latter embellished the interiors of at least two buildings in London, one in Belsize Park, the other in Hendon. This was an exacting technique in which speed and skill are essential, since the design is painted directly onto wet plaster and must be completed before the plaster dries. Jackson also did a painting in tempera of St George for the church of Great Harwood in Northamptonshire for which Dorothy Hutton provided a gold background. Although he experimented in fresco and distemper, most of his work in the revived techniques was done in tempera [41].

In his youth, Jackson had done a number of portraits in oil. The first work he exhibited at the Royal Academy in London in 1907 was an oil painting of his future wife, Gertrude Templeton, but from 1900 to c.1920, his work in portraiture was confined mainly to lithographs. In the 1920s, however, he sometimes did versions of the same sitter in lithography and in oil or in lithography and in tempera, such as those of the politician, Andrew McLaren, M.P. (exhibited RA 1923), and the industrialist, Laurence Pilkington (exhibited RA 1924). Jackson's daughter, who became a favourite model, appears in a Raphaelesque full face portrait in c.1921 (cat. 41), and again, in *Betty with Tulips* (cat. 50), a softer and more imposing portrait which was awarded a medal at the Paris Salon of 1929. He also painted at least two self-portraits, one head and shoulders (cat. 53), and the other showing him with brush in hand, painting a picture of still-life, which he presented to the Art Workers' Guild. In his later years, portraits in oil become more common. In addition to his many portrait commissions, he also drew and painted portraits of his friends and students: Elsie Henderson, Dorothy Hutton, Janet Cree, Anne Newland, Lindsay Gladstone as well as the devoted secretary of the Byam Shaw School, Pamela Ovens.

While Jackson's experiments with different painting media were uniformly successful, his work as a draughtsman and lithographer and his career as a teacher were all of more importance than his work as a painter. He found difficulty in uniting his draughtsmanship with an effective

---

40. According to Anna Hornby, an early portrait of Betty is based on a painting by Raphael in Bergamo (Ovens).
41. Charles Stewart recalls that Cennini's handbook was a standard text-book in the painting class.

composition. His fine taste and impeccable talent for drawing in the classical tradition should have destined him to paint subject pictures in the tradition of the Great Masters. Early in his career, he tried to paint in the idyllic style of Charles Shannon, but such poetry was not in his nature. Jackson lacked the power of invention which is essential in figure composition. This is probably why he concentrated on portraits, still-life paintings and landscapes. George Warner Allen recalled that Jackson tried to make his pupils draw like Raphael and paint like an Impressionist. In his later years, Jackson's own work divides along similar lines and he produced a number of landscapes and still-life paintings in an attractive Impressionist style which make no use of his superb talent for figure drawing. As paintings, however, these are much more successful than the Shannonesque works.

Jackson was involved in many different types of organizations connected with art and art education. In addition to his involvement in the Senefelder Club and in the Tempera Society he joined the Art Workers' Guild in 1916, becoming one of its most distinguished Masters in 1928. In 1915, together with Ambrose Heal, whose portrait he painted, and others, he helped to found The Design and Industries Association, whose purpose was to encourage good draughtsmanship and design in British industry. Appointed to the faculties of engraving and painting at the British School in Rome, he eventually became chairman of the Painting Faculty. His important role in hanging the exhibition of Flemish painting at the Royal Academy in 1927 led to his being decorated by the Belgian state and becoming a member of the Académie des Beaux-Arts in Antwerp.

However, the peak of Jackson's career came in 1926 when he took over the Byam Shaw School in Campden St, near Notting Hill. Since 1921, he had been teaching life drawing there but once he took over as Principal, he gave up all his other teaching jobs except for his post at the Royal Academy Schools. He taught three days at the Byam Shaw and two evenings at the Royal Academy, leaving two days for his own work. As Principal of the School from 1926 to 1940, "Jacky", as he was called behind his back, was in his element, inspiring awe, affection and achievement in his students. For him, the days at Campden St were his happiest even though his concentration on teaching meant that his own artistic output was now relatively small. Like the R.A. Schools under Charles Sims, the Royal College under William Rothenstein and the Slade under Legros and his followers, the Byam Shaw under Jackson emphasised conservative values, based on the tradition of the Paris studios. As generations of artists had done before, his students began by drawing from plaster casts where the interpretative selection from nature made by the earlier masters facilitated their task. They then moved on to the life-class and finally, when Jackson deemed them ready, to the "Head Room". Whereas other art schools were throwing out principles of academic draughtsmanship along with their plaster casts and embracing the tenets of the modern movements, Jackson's lessons in sound drawing continued to be the foundation of the Byam Shaw into the 1960s. As Brian Thomas pointed out, Jackson was "less concerned with novelty than with excellence" [42]. Other like-minded artists and friends like Ricketts, Shannon and Glyn Philpot would come in to talk to the students, to criticize their work or to hand out prizes. Shannon also taught there for a few years. Philpot, who was Visitor to the School for a

---

42. B. Thomas, *The Burlington Magazine*, 88 (Nov 1946), p. 279.

number of years, offered a prize of five pounds "as an encouragement for figure composition" [43]. Ricketts gave a private scholarship of two hundred pounds to Max Chapman, one of Jackson's students, whose accomplished drawings had failed to win the Prix de Rome, despite all the efforts of Ricketts who was on the selection committee.

It is remarkable that this small private school, in competition with all the other art schools in the country, should in one decade have produced two winners of the Prix de Rome, then the most coveted art prize in Britain: Richard Finny (1929) and Brian Thomas (1934). On two other occasions, students from the Byam Shaw were runners up. Another student, Anne Newland, won the Abbey Scholarship in 1938 and works by two other students, Janet Cree and Eliot Hodgkin, were purchased by the Chantrey Bequest in 1933 and 1936. As Jackson himself liked to point out, these students had only received three or four years of training in contrast with the five or more enjoyed by many of the competitors. His achievement was warmly acknowledged in C.R.W. Nevinson's autobiography: "Of all the men I have met who deal with the teaching of art, [Jackson] is the finest and most erudite: a technician and an artist. No wonder he is now in charge of one of the best art schools in the world. Many letters reach me from parents asking for advice about art and art students and ... I always recommend the Byam Shaw school for young people who have any real talent" [44]. Artists as various as Tuke, Tonks, Philpot, Orpen and Anning Bell did likewise.

With the Second World War, both the Byam Shaw and the R.A. Schools were forced to close and Jackson, aged sixty-six, was left without work or income. The purchase in 1940 by the Chantrey Bequest of his portrait of Mrs Beesley, a professional model, for one hundred pounds, brought some consolation. After completing a series of nine portraits of war heroes in the Admiralty and War Ordnance Factory and spending a dispiriting three years in camouflage at Leamington, he eventually settled in Oxford. However, there was something "missing in this lovely city, there is no Campden Street! I sometimes think it all a dream – that I could not ever have been so happy as I was in that little street". Ironically, now that he had no longer any need to teach, he had more time for his own work and these last years were his most prolific. From Oxford, he visited friends and old students and did many drawings and paintings of the city and of the surrounding villages and countryside. The titles of the paintings exhibited at his Memorial Exhibition reveal his peregrinations in the vicinity: *Binsey, Oxford, Shillingford, Hambleden Weir, Clifton Hampden, The Thames near Moulsford* and *The Thames near Mapledurham*. He was also painting pictures of still-life as well as portraits which involved even wider displacement. "I am doing portraits & travelling about more than I like to do", he wrote in a letter to his students, "but needs must when the devil drives. Slough, Birmingham, Manchster, Guildford & where next I know not" [45]. In fact, he had more commissions than he could cope with.

One of his last portraits was of the magnificently bearded Nicholas Gibbs, a Scottish Abbot in the Greek Orthodox Church. In addition to the painting of Gibbs, Jackson did at least two

---

43. Glyn Philpot to Jackson, 14 June 1928 (private collection).
44. C. R. W. Nevinson, *Paint and Prejudice*, p. 54.
45. The letter, dated 12 May 1944, was one of several circulated among his students, with Pamela Ovens and others adding their news as it went from address to address.

preparatory drawings in *deux crayons* (cat. 72), using two different colours of chalk, a technique which Jackson often used. The painting of the Abbot and one of the related drawings were exhibited at the Royal Academy in 1944 and 1945. These were among the last of Jackson's works to be shown at the R.A.

Jackson exhibited his first work at the Royal Academy in 1907 but only began exhibiting regularly there after 1920. In April 1944, he finally became an A.R.A. His pleasure in his election was enhanced by the fact that it had finally come as a tribute from his peers and without any lobbying on his part. This was an honour he had refused on an earlier occasion when several Academicians wished to recognize the successful changes which he had introduced to the teaching of drawing at the Royal Academy Schools. Now, he enjoyed working with "a body of whose full beneficence he said the public had no idea" [46]. No doubt he would soon have been elected to full membership in the Academy had he not been struck by a motor-cycle as he was crossing the street near Magdalen Bridge. He died a few days later on 11 March 1945.

During his life, Jackson had never held a one-man show but he always included work at the exhibitions of the societies of which he was a member, such as the annual shows of the Senefelder Club and the less frequent ones of the Tempera Society. Even before he had become a regular exhibitor at the Royal Academy, he had sent work every year to the Paris Salon from 1909 onwards. In all these exhibitions, however, he was represented by only a few works among those of many artists. As a result, the Memorial Exhibition, held at the Beaux Arts Gallery at the end of 1946 was the first occasion where all his work in different media was exhibited together. His superb drawings, his lithographs, his watercolours, his paintings in oil, in tempera, in distemper and in true fresco, his portraits, his still-life paintings and the many landscapes from his last years not only gave an overview of his career but showed his high level of achievement in each form. A monument to him was erected in St James's Church, Piccadilly, where many English artists are commemorated. This was paid for by his former students, fellow artists and friends. The original intention was to hang his *Pietà* over the side altar on the right. According to George Warner Allen, the plan was opposed by a church official on the grounds that Christ's navel might distract the faithful at prayer and it was eventually set up in its present location on the wall beside the memorial.

After the war, a group of Jackson's students and the school's former secretary, Pamela Ovens, re-established the Byam Shaw and ran it according to Jackson's principles. Ovens purchased the school and became its Director while Brian Dick Lauder Thomas, known to his friends as "Dick", and Patrick Phillips (1907-1976) became joint Principals. Thomas had been Jackson's star pupil and heir apparent. A winner of the Prix de Rome, he was a marvellous draughtsman and a very able teacher and administrator. In a letter written to him in 1935, Jackson had expressed the wish that he and Phillips might eventually succeed him: "I often wish that someone like you and say Phillips would consider the idea of gradually taking over the Byam Shaw School from me" [47]. Phillips had studied under Jackson from 1926-30 and was also an excellent draughtsman. As he

46. B. Thomas, *The Burlington Magazine*, 88 (1946), p. 280
47. Jackson to Brian Thomas, 13 June 1945 (Ovens).

had been teaching at the school since 1933, he helped to provide a bridge to the pre-war period. Most of the teachers who were taken on after the war – Peter Greenham, Bernard Dunstan, Charles Stewart and George Warner Allen – had also been trained by Jackson and were able to continue teaching the principles of drawing and the artistic values which they had learned from him.

The most famous of Jackson's pupils was Peter Greenham, RA (1909–92). After working as a schoolmaster for a few years, Greenham went to the Slade to study art but left after five days in order to study at the Byam Shaw. His brother, Robert, who had studied under Jackson at the RA Schools, had assured him that Jackson was "the only man in England who could teach drawing". Under him, Greenham felt that his needs were at last recognized. Although he developed a painting style very different from his master's, the sound draughtsmanship which he had learned from him underlies all his portraits and landscapes. Greenham always readily acknowledged Jackson's importance in his artistic development and continued to stress the Jacksonian principles of good drawing after he had been appointed Keeper of the Royal Academy Schools in 1964. At the time of Jackson's death, he wrote a warm tribute in his memory.

Robert Greenham (1906–1992) had already begun his prize-winning career when his brother followed him to the Byam Shaw. His manner of drawing was more linear and his landscapes more stylized than Peter's, in keeping with a decorative element which is commonly found in the art of the 1920s, particularly among the muralists. Jackson's own art was tending to become less stylized and less archaic in this period but the influence of Ricketts and Glyn Philpot at the School no doubt sustained the pupils' interest in the role of linear composition.

Brian Thomas (1912–89) and George Warner Allen (1916–99), known as "les deux neutres" because of their ascetic devotion to art, were particularly interested in the element of design. Thomas, who had the greater gifts and facility of the two, soon realised that there was no future for the classical tradition in painting and moved to the decorative arts where stained glass and architectural decoration still offered a viable career for the academically trained artist. He did a number of very important commissions, including a mural for Lambeth Palace and windows for Westminster Abbey, St Paul's Cathedral, St George's Chapel, Windsor and Wellington Cathedral in New Zealand. He had a taste for committees and was an active figure behind the scenes in the world of British art. Like Jackson, he became Master of the Art Workers' Guild.

Warner Allen, on the other hand, stubbornly continued to paint large religious and mythological works in a style that was completely out of keeping with current developments in art. Although he had a successful exhibition in London in 1952 his distaste for contemporary art left him increasingly isolated. His work in camouflage during the war had developed his interest in the scientific analysis of Old Master paintings and he painted in a mixed medium of oil and tempera which he believed had been used by Titian. For each painting, he did elaborate preparatory drawings, a cartoon and an underpainting. With the recent revival of interest in figurative painting, he was represented after many years of lonely obscurity, by two major paintings in the *Last Romantics* show at the Barbican in 1989. Two of his works are now in the Tate Gallery.

---

48. Quoted on the back flap of the cover of *Ernest Jackson Drawings and Lithographs.*

Eliot Hodgkin (1905–87), who had studied under Jackson at both the Byam Shaw and the RA Schools, shared Warner Allen's interest in tempera. His exquisite still-life pictures of fruit and flowers in this medium are his best known works but he also worked in oil and did landscapes and murals. He once told Jackson that he remembered "often & carefully" the things which Jackson had taught him: "I know that anything good I may do in drawing or painting comes from what you told me" [49].

Charles Stewart (b.1915), who attended the Byam Shaw School from 1932 to 1938, confined his student work to drawing and went on to become an elegant illustrator of books published by the Limited Editions Club of America and the Folio Society. His work exemplifies the immaculate standard of drawing achieved at the school under Jackson which continued when Stewart and his fellow students returned as teachers at the school after the war. Like several of the most successful of Jackson's pupils, he has made his reputation outside the mainstream of British twentieth-century art by concentrating in the more ornamental branches: book illustration, costume design, landscape and still-life. These art forms offered a livelihood for draughtsmen trained in a classic tradition which no longer interested the grand patrons of contemporary art and has passed into extinction in the art schools. Charles Stewart's costume collection now forms a museum of costume at New Abbey near Dumfries.

Perhaps the most surprising of Jackson's followers was Pamela Ovens (1903–85) who revealed her talent in painting only after she had left the directorship of the school in 1962. In her youth, she had wanted to become an artist but had studied physiology at Oxford. As secretary at the Byam Shaw, she effectively ran the school, leaving Jackson to take care of the artistic side. However, unknown to the students, she quietly absorbed Jackson's lessons and after retiring to Italy, began to produce lovely landscapes in wash and in oil which were very much in the Byam Shaw tradition. On returning to London, she regularly took painting holidays in Italy and the South of France until her tragic death in 1985 when she was struck by a taxi.

Just before the war, at the time of the Munich crisis, George Warner Allen turned to Jackson (who was sitting on the floor of the antique room during a rest period from hanging the school exhibition) and remarked: "Wouldn't it be wonderful, Sir, to have lived in a world where one could produce the Raphael frescoes". "I know, I know, Allen", Jackson replied, "but keep the place warm, keep the place warm." This is what Jackson himself did in keeping alive the classical tradition of drawing and in passing this on to his students at a time when the art world was increasingly hostile to these values.

---

49. Eliot Hodgkin to Jackson, 8 May (Ovens).

CATALOGUE
compiled by Jon Whiteley

Plate 1

Plate 2

1. *La Toilette* (pl. 1)
silverpoint on smooth greyish paper,
torn along upper edge
177:126 mm
verso: *figure seated on a stool*
Presented by Charles Stewart 1997.53
From a sketchbook of c. 1904. The motif recalls works by Degas and Puvis de Chavannes. The technique of metalpoint drawing was revived in the later nineteenth century, particularly by Legros, at a time of renewed interest in the drawings of the Early Renaissance.

2. *Portrait of Miss Hutchings*
silverpoint on smooth white card prepared with grey
wash   343:260 mm
inscribed in graphite lower right: *Miss Hutchings/D30 (Mrs Vale)*. Lent from a private collection

3. *Mrs Godwin* (pl. 2)
black crayon on off-white card   279:268 mm
Lent by Dr J.G.P.Delaney.
Drawn in 1909 in a broken, dotted manner somewhat similar to Sickert's.

Plate 3

4. *Portrait of Gertrude Anne Templeton* (pl. 3)
oil on canvas
565:460 mm
inscribed in red paint lower right: *F.E.J*
Lent from a private collection.

Painted shortly before the sitter's marriage to Jackson in 1910. Gertrude Templeton was a professional singer and actress. She met Jackson while working for Beerbohm Tree's company at the His Majesty's Theatre in the Haymarket where he was involved in designing sets.

Plate 4

5. *Lithographic tools* (pl. 4)
red chalk with pen and black ink and grey and brown
wash, touched with white bodycolour on beige wove
paper   280:327 mm
Lent from a private collection.

6. *The Buccaneer* (pl. 5)
lithograph printed in dark brown with scratching out
on thin white wove paper
285:230 mm (stone)
inscribed on the stone, lower left: *F.E.J.* over erased
inscription: and again in graphite, lower right:
F. Ernest Jackson.
Lent by Dr J.G.P. Delaney.
Exhibited at the Paris Salon in 1909 along with no. 7.
The use of scratching in lithography was disputed by
Jackson's fellow print-makers but the practice of drawing
directly on the stone lends itself to this technique and
Jackson used it frequently in his early prints.
The Buccaneer *was reproduced in* The Studio *in 1904*
and must be approximately contemporary.

Plate 5

Plate 6

7. *The Black Hat* (pl. 6)
lithograph printed in black on thin laid paper
565:482 mm
inscribed in graphite lower centre: *F. Ernest Jackson del et imp.*
Lent from a private collection.
A portrait of the Gertrude Templeton, drawn in c.1909, before her marriage to Jackson in 1910.

8. *The Profile: Mrs Gertude Anne Jackson seated holding a book* (pl. 7)
etching
190:198 mm (plate);280:290 mm (sheet)
Lent from a private collection.
Etched in about 1911. Following her marriage which marked the end of her theatrical career, Mrs Jackson took lessons in bookbinding from Sidney Cockerell. She became an accomplished bookbinder until ill-health prevented her from continuing.

Plate 7

9. *La Robe de Velours* (pl. 8)
lithograph printed in black on off-white wove paper
275:240 mm (image); 325:253 mm (sheet)
inscribed in graphite below: *F. Ernest Jackson imp.*
Lent by Dr J.G.P. Delaney.
Exhibited at the Paris Salon in 1911 together with no. 10. These were singled out by the reviewer of the Gazette des Beaux-Arts as two of the finest lithographs at the exhibition. In both prints, the artist combines scratching and rubbing with delicate linear touches of a sharp lithographic crayon to create magical effects of light which enhance the air of melancholy in the sitter's face.

Plate 8

Plate 9

12. *Evening Snow in London* (pl. 10)
lithograph printed in blue and black
160:180 mm (image);380:480 mm (sheet)
Lent from a private collection.
Printed in four differently coloured states, this is one of Jackson's most atmospheric lithographs. The site is indentified on the backboard as Bedford Square where the Jacksons lived in a top flat at no. 47 before moving to Chiswick, in 1913. This, however, does not seem to represent Bedford Square. In a letter of 1949, Elsie Henderson described it as a view in Kensington. As Jackson lived at 1a Phillimore Gardens in Kensington before his marriage, addresses may have been confused.

13. Evening Snow in London
lithograph printed in pale blue and beige on stiff off-white wove paper
160:180 mm (image); 380:480 mm (sheet)
One of four colour combinations used in printing this lithograph.

14. *Alix Sargant Florence*
lithograph printed in black on thin off-white wove paper
290:247 mm (stone: lower right corner missing); 358:319 mm (sheet)
Lent by Dr J.G.P. Delaney.
One of two portraits commissioned by the artist, Mary Florence Sargent, of her children, Alix and Philip (no. 15), in c.1912.

10. *Effet de Lumière* (pl. 9)
lithograph printed in black on stiff, pale cream paper, trimmed and inserted into a copy of the *Gazette des Beaux-Arts.*
211:190 mm (image); 270:190 mm (sheet)
scratched signature upper left: *F E Jackson*
Lent by the Ashmolean Library
Exhibited at the Salon of 1911 with the Robe de Velours *(cat. 9). An edition of* Effet de Lumière *was printed for the* Gazette *and bound into the July issue.*

11. *Vase of roses*
lithograph in black on thin cream laid paper
350:270 mm (stone); 452:315 mm(sheet)
Lent from a private collection.

Plate 10

15. *Philip Sargant Florence* (pl. 11)
lithograph printed in black with erasures on coarse
beige paper; some trial touches upper left.
345:266 mm (stone: damaged centre left);
505:320 mm (sheet)
inscribed in graphite lower left: *Philip Sargant
Florence*
Lent by Dr J.G.P. Delaney.

16. *Portrait of David Don*
lithograph printed in black on pale cream laid paper
226:165 mm (stone); 325:253 mm (sheet)
signed in graphite below: *F. Ernest Jackson*
Lent by Dr J.G.P. Delaney.

17. *Bill*
lithograph printed in black on off-white wove
paper
345:285 mm; 485:322 mm (sheet)
inscribed in graphite lower right: *F Ernest Jackson imp*
Lent by Dr J.G.P. Delaney
Printed in c. 1911 when it was shown at the N.E.A.C.

Plate 12

Plate 11

18. *Mrs Emmanuel*
lithograph printed in black on off-white wove paper
320:270 mm approx. (stone); 447:282 mm (sheet)
inscribed in graphite, lower left: *Mrs Emmanuel*
Lent by Dr J.G.P. Delaney.
*The second, darker tone added in the hair is patterned
with the impression of paper or textile.*

19. *The Old Model* (pl. 12)
lithograph printed in black on crisp, off-white laid
paper   352:275 mm (stone); 434:302 mm (sheet)
inscribed lower left: *The Old Model*
wm: a unicorn and initials: FJH
Lent by Dr J.G.P. Delaney.

20. *The Garden*
lithograph printed in black on white laid paper
300:260 mm (image); 480:360 mm (sheet)
inscribed in graphite lower right: *F. Ernest Jackson
imp*; and on lower left: *No. 16/20*
Lent from a private collection.

Plate 13

21. *Chiswick Mall at Stamford Brook* (pl. 13)
lithograph printed in black on heavyweight cream
wove paper
775:525 mm (image); 980:683 mm (sheet)
signed on the stone, lower right: *F. Ernest Jackson
artist's proof*
Lent by Dr J.G.P. Delaney.
*Proof state of the first of four posters designed by Jackson
for The London Electric Railway (the present Underground). The view, drawn in 1913, is taken from
Morton House in Chiswick Mall where Jackson had
moved recently from Bedford Square. In 1919, the
Jacksons moved into a smaller house in Chiswick Mall
where they remained until 1940.*

22. *The Church of St Riquier*
lithograph printed in black on off-white wove
paper   370:260 mm (image); 495:365 mm (plate)
Lent by Dr J.G.P. Delaney
*An impression of this print was given to the each of the
lay-members (non-artists) of the Senefelder Club in
1913.*

23. *Four studies of an arm and one of a hand*
red chalk touched with black chalk on off-white
antique laid paper   245:334 mm
inscribed in graphite lower right: *D 48 Study for
England and France.*
Lent from a private collection.
*One of a number of early studies drawn in the manner
of Watteau. The arm studies are preparatory variants,
reversed by the printing process, for the upraised arm of
France in no. 24. The hand, also in reverse, relates to
the figure of England.*

24. *Defence against Aggression: England and France*
(pl. 14)
lithograph printed in pink, green, black and yellow
on white wove paper   795:505 mm
Lent from a private collection.
*Proof state of a poster commissioned by the Ministry of
Information in support of the war effort. The figure of
France is inspired by a lithograph after Puvis de
Chavanne's painting,* The Carrier Pigeon, *one of two
prints after works by Puvis published in 1870 in support
of the Red Cross.*

Plate 14

Plate 15

25. *View of Lambeth Palace* (pl. 15)
lithograph printed in beige, dull pink, two tones of
blue, green and grey on off-white wove paper; the
inscription *The Palace of Lambeth* and the arms of the
Bishop of London are added in watercolour on a sheet
of paper mounted separately below.
690:830 mm

Lent from a private collection.
*One of a number of lithographs commissioned from
artists by the London County Council for the city
schools. Jackson was put in charge of the undertaking.
The artist's daughter recalls sitting beside her father in
1918 in a barge moored on the opposite bank while he
made the preparatory drawing.*

26. *Head of a woman* (pl. 16)
lithograph printed in red on off-white wove paper
392:312 mm
inscribed in graphite, lower right:
The Refugee, lithograph
Lent from a private collection.
*Probably drawn during a visit to Rouen during the First
World War. The print, which is deceptively like a
drawing in red chalk, was exhibited at the Senefelder
Club in 1919.*

27. *The Release* (pl. 17)
colour lithograph on white wove paper
205:150 mm
Lent from a private collection.
Inspired by The Balloon, *one of two lithographs drawn
in 1870 by Vernier after a painting by Puvis de
Chavannes. No. 24 was similarly inspired by the
companion print,* The Carrier Pigeon. *Jackson would
have been attracted to Puvis as a member of the Société
des Artistes Français Lithographes established by Henri
Hamel in the 1890s for the purpose of reviving artistic
lithography in France. Charles Stewart recalls that
Jackson often recommended the work of Puvis to his
students. The print dates from c. 1919.*

Plate 18

28. *Sweet Williams* (pl. 18)
lithograph printed in yellow, green, blue, ochre and
red   170:150 mm (image); 360:320 mm (sheet)
Lent from a private collection.
inscribed in graphite lower left: *trial proof;* and in
lower right: *FEJ*
*Printed in c.1919. The simple unshaded image allowed
the artist scope for skilful colour printing.*

29. *Portrait of Henry Festing Jones*
red and black chalk on white wove paper
358:238 mm (sight)
Lent by Dr J.G.P. Delaney.
*One of at least two preparatory drawings made
for no. 30.*

30. *Portrait of Henry Festing Jones*
brush and crayon lithograph printed in black
350:210 mm (image).
Lent by Dr J.G.P. Delaney.
One of Jackson's later lithographs, published in Vogue
*magazine on 17 March 1921. The bold use of litho-
graphic ink dramatically alters the effect of the study on
which Jackson based the print. As the head is printed in
the same direction as the drawing, the artist must have
used an intermediary process to draw a reversed image
on the stone.*

Plate 16

F Ernest Jackson. imp.

Plate 17

Plate 19

31. *Portrait of John Burns*
red chalk on thick beige paper   395:290 mm
signed in red chalk lower right: *Ernest Jackson/ 1920*

32. *Head of a girl*
red chalk with some added black chalk on off-white
paper prepared with gesso and washed with pink
382:308 mm (irregular)
Lent from a private collection.
*The use of hard, grainy gesso as a ground for red chalk
must have made it difficult to draw in neat contours but
would have helped the artist to dissolve the strokes of
chalk in areas of liquid modelling.*

33. *Allée des Marmoutiers*
etching printed in black on heavy, hand-made wove
paper   150:100 mm (plate); 238:161 mm (sheet)
Lent by Dr J.G.P. Delaney.
*Probably derived from one of several drawings and
watercolours of the palace gardens of Versailles made by
Jackson in c. 1911.*

34. *View of the gardens at Versailles* (pl. 19)
watercolour on grey paper   260:198 mm
Lent from a private collection.
*Drawn in c.1911. The view shows Desjardins' statue of
Diana.*

35. *View of a fountain in the gardens at Versailles*
watercolour on grey paper with pin holes in each
corner   395:263 mm
Lent from a private collection.

36. *An archway in the church of Saint-Ours at Loches*
graphite and watercolour on white paper
585:465 mm
inscribed in graphite lower right: *F. Ernest Jackson/
1911.*
Lent from a private collection.
*Jackson's watercolour records the traces of ancient colour
which remain on the sculptures of the arch.*

37. *View of a gate-house at Caen* (pl. 20)
graphite with brown wash on white laid paper
200:249 mm
inscribed in graphite, lower right: *Caen July 1920*
Presented by Charles Stewart 1997.75
Probably drawn on a family holiday in Normandy.

38. *Portrait of Betty Jackson in profile*
oil and tempera on canvas   450:375 mm
Lent from a private collection.
A version of no. 39.

Plate 20

Plate 21

41. *Portrait of Betty Jackson* (pl. 22)
oil and tempera on board
215:195 mm
Lent from a private collection.
Anna Hornby recalled that an early portrait of Betty Jackson was based on a painting by Raphael in Bergamo. This must be Raphael's head of St Sebastian which has a clear affinity with the present portrait. The townscape in the background is appropriately Italianate. The painting dates from 1921. The artist painted a similar portrait of Miss Jackson in tempera in 1924 (see no. 48).

42. *Dorothy Hutton in profile reading*
pen and black ink on thin off-white paper
226:197 mm
wm: ..EY CONGRESS LINEN BOND 1914
Lent from a private collection.
One of at least two pen drawings of the same model with a book drawn in c.1920, probably in connexion with The Manuscript *(no. 43).*

39. *Portrait of Betty Jackson with a red bow*
egg tempera and gold paint on vellum
140:100 mm
Lent from a private collection.
Painted in 1917 when the sitter was four and a half. One of the earliest known instances of the artist's use of egg tempera, a medium which he continued to use into the 1920s. The sharp profile, bright colour and flattened treatment of the patterned costume are inspired by fifteenth-century Italian portraits.

40. *Portrait of Pen Goldman (Commander Penryn Monk)* (pl. 21)
egg tempera and gold paint on vellum
205:150 mm
Lent from a private collection.
Painted in 1917 for the sitter's foster mother who asked for a portrait in the manner of Betty with a red bow *(no. 39).*

Plate 22

Plate 23

43. *The Manuscript* (pl. 23)
egg tempera on panel
288:341 mm (sight)
Bequeathed by Anna Hornby 1996.34
The subject represents the artist, Dorothy Hutton,
painted in c. 1921.

44. *Girl seated with an open book* (pl. 24)
egg tempera with added oil on plywood
260:205 mm
Lent from a private collection.
A variant of the theme of no. 43. The background was
overpainted with grey oil by Peter Greenham.

45. *Portrait of Dorothy Hutton*
oil on canvas
510:410 mm
Lent from a private collection.
Dorothy Hutton (1889-1984) studied at the Central
School of Arts and Crafts under Jackson. She exhibited
flower paintings but was also an illustrator and scribe.

Plate 24

Plate 25

46. *Study of a cat* (pl. 25)
brown conté crayon on thin white paper serrated
along upper edge
94:130 mm
inscribed in graphite lower right: *F.E.J.*
Lent from a private collection.
*One of many studies of the artist's cat, Timothy, taken
from a note-book or note-books used by the artist in the
1920s.*

47. *Four studies of a sleeping cat*
soft graphite on thin off-white wove paper
149:128 mm
inscribed in graphite lower centre: *FE.J.*
Lent from a private collection.

Plate 26

50. *Portrait of Betty with Tulips* (pl. 27)
oil on canvas
755:620 mm
Lent from a private collection.
*Miss Jackson's costume was devised for a fancy dress
party at which she was dressed as a Dutch girl. The
painting was executed on consecutive weekends in the
time left after the week's teaching commitments had been
met. The painting was awarded a silver medal at the
Paris Salon of 1929.*

51. *Sleeping model*
graphite on off-white wove paper
216:320 mm
Lent from a private collection.

52. *Head of a female model*
red chalk with touches of black chalk
on beige laid paper
462:315 mm
Lent from a private collection.

48. *Study of Betty Jackson* (pl. 26)
red and blue chalks over graphite on wove paper
390:288 mm
Lent from a private collection.
*Jackson often drew heads in red chalk and touched in
the details with a secondary colour, generally black. The
head is similar to the painting of Betty of c.1921 but
was drawn about three years later for another portrait in
tempera.*

49. *Portrait of Monsieur Soetmus*
red chalk on beige paper
355:270 mm
Lent from a private collection.
*The sitter's name is given in an inscription on the
backboard.*

Plate 27

Plate 28

40

53. *Self-portrait* (pl. 28)
oil on canvas
555:385 mm
Lent from a private collection.
Painted with the broader touch which Jackson used
mainly in his later work. The artist thought that his
features seemed uncharacteristically grim; but, according
to his daughter, the portrait accurately represents his
expression of concentration while working at the easel.

54. *Female nude, seated, leaning to right* (pl. 29)
red chalk on pale cream paper, cut along upper edge
185:215 mm
Presented by Charles Stewart 1997.55
Nos 54 to 59 are demonstration drawings done for
Charles Stewart who was a student at the Byam Shaw
School from 1932 to 1938.

55. *Half-length reclining male nude*
graphite on pale cream paper, laid down on card
140:205 mm (irregular)
Presented by Charles Stewart 1997.64

56. *A woman's head turned to right*
graphite on pale cream paper
99:78 mm
fragmentary inscription upper left, cut off.
Presented by Charles Stewart 1997.67

57. *Study of a woman's dress with a faint indication of*
a woman standing on right
brown chalk (on the dress) and graphite (on the
figure) on pale cream paper
299:178 mm
Presented by Charles Stewart 1997.57

58. *Study of a woman's dress*
graphite with pink wash on cream paper
317:125 mm
Presented by Charles Stewart 1997.58

59. *A woman, wearing a long-sleeved dress, seen*
three-quarters from behind (pl. 30)
graphite with blue and greenish-blue washes on cream
paper
365:212 mm
Presented by Charles Stewart 1997.59
The dress was a sapphire blue satin theatrical costume
from the school drapery cupboard. Jackson used a version
of it in his lithograph The Release.

Plate 29

Plate 30

41

Plate 31

Plate 32

60. *Head of a male model* (pl. 31)
graphite and red chalk on off-white card
380:297 mm
Lent from a private collection.

61. *Head study in profile*
red chalk on laid paper   180:170 mm
Lent from a private collection.
Drawn for Mrs Mary Edmonds, née Baldwin, in 1934.

62. *"Jonathan".*
graphite, pen and black ink on two pieces of off-white
paper, mounted on card   302:234 mm
inscribed in graphite lower left: *7 June 1940*
Bequeathed by Anna Hornby 1996.32
*Demonstration drawing made for Anna Hornby at the
Byam Shaw in 1940 from one of the professional models
employed at the school.*

63. *Album of studies mostly by Jackson*
52 folios of coarse green paper bound in brown
boards   555:375 mm
Lent from a private collection.
*The album consists mainly of studies drawn by Jackson
for Dorothy Spofforth and other studies drawn by herself
and corrected by Jackson while she was a student at the
Byam Shaw School. As the artist was deaf, Jackson
communicated with her in writing. She transcribed
extracts from his letters and from her diary onto slips of
paper and inserted them into the album beside the
studies. The album provides a useful running commen-
tary on the development of a pupil's work from 1934 to
1940 and a valuable record of Jackson's teaching. The
album is open at a study of a nude, dated 1940 with the
comment: "Painter's Drawing/ Finding things and losing
things". There is little contour and the modelling is done
with much rubbing and scribbling.*

64. *Head study of a man with a hat* (pl. 32)
oil on card
350:260 mm
Lent from a private collection.
Nos 64 and 65 were painted as demonstration studies in the Head Class for Bruyère Marriott in c. 1936. The Head Class was the most advanced of the stages through which the student at the Byam Shaw passed.

65. *Head study of a man with blue turban*
oil on card
360:260 mm
Lent from a private collection.

66. *Head study of a girl wearing a red cap*
oil on card
355:250 mm
Lent from a private collection.
A demonstration piece painted in the Head Class in c 1936.

Plate 34

Plate 33

67. *Head of a charwoman* (pl. 33)
oil on board   355:255 mm
scratched inscription lower right: *EJ*
Lent from a private collection.
Demonstrating the relation of reflected light and colour in the shaded areas of the head to the lighter parts.

68. *Portrait of a woman in profile working at an easel*
pen and black ink on a page removed from a register and cut in half   175:200 mm
inscribed in graphite upper left: *D74 Girl's head*; and in pen and brown ink, upper right: *16*
Lent from a private collection.

69. *Study of a girl seated facing right*
red chalk on beige laid paper   315:244 mm
inscribed in graphite lower right: *Girl sitting D52*
Lent from a private collection.

70. *Portrait of Lindsay Gladstone* (pl. 34)
oil on canvas   514:410 mm
Bequeathed by Anna Hornby 1996.35
Painted c. 1940. The sitter studied at the Byam Shaw School under Jackson in the late 1930s.

Plate 35

71. *Portrait of a woman looking to the right*
red and black chalks on off-white laid paper
315:240 mm
inscribed in red chalk upper right: *Kingston Bagpuize/*
[illegible]
wm: I D v d B
Lent from a private collection.
*Probably drawn in the mid-1940s after Jackson had
retired to Oxford.*

72. *Head study of the Archimandrite Nicholas* (pl. 35)
black and white chalks on cream card backing of a
portrait photograph   406:330 mm
Lent from a private collection.
*A study of 1943 for a painted portrait exhibited at the
Royal Academy in 1945. The sitter, Nicholas Gibbs,
was the Scottish-born superior of a Greek Orthodox
monastic community.*

73. *View of Magdalen College tower*
oil on plywood   255:360 mm
Lent from a private collection.
*Painted in 1944. The view is taken from Magdalen
College School playground.*

74. *View of Chertsey Bridge*
oil on pasteboard   255:355 mm
Lent from a private collection.
Painted in about 1945.

JACKSON'S PUPILS:

George Warner Allen (1916–1988)

75. *Two studies of a woman's head*
graphite and red chalk on stiff cream wove paper
383: 275 mm
inscribed in graphite, lower left: *Mrs Butcher George
Warner Allen*
Presented by Dr J.G.P. Delaney 2000.9

76. *Judas*
graphite with grey and black washes, heightened with
white bodycolour on cream wove paper
525:340 mm (irregular)
Presented by Dr J.G.P. Delaney 2000.12

*A full size model for a painting on panel. The sheet is
extensively inscribed with notes relating to the size of the
final painting. Although the artist was a self-conscious
traditionalist there is an atmospheric quality in his
treatment of the theme which recalls the dream-like
character of contemporary Surrealism.*

77. *Studies for two paintings*
black chalk, squared in graphite   377:558 mm
Presented by Dr J.G.P. Delaney 2000.13
*Advanced studies for paintings illustrating Matthew
Arnold's* The Scholar Gipsy *(left) and* Thyrsus *(right).*

Peter Greenham (1909–1992)

78. *The American Boy*
oil on canvas
505:610 mm
Lent from a private collection.
Peter Greenham acquired his life-long mastery of drawing at the Byam Shaw School which he attended from 1936 to 1939. In 1954, he joined the teaching staff at the Royal Academy Schools, basing his classes on Jackson's lessons at the Byam Shaw. Like Jackson, he taught by demonstration. This portrait was painted as a demonstration for a class of students at Choate School, Wallingford near Yale, in 1966.

Joan Hassall (1906–1988)

79. *Six prints*
woodengravings (one corrected with added white)
Presented by Arthur Mitchell, 1964
Proof states for four illustrations in Mary Russell Mitford's Our Village, *published by George G. Harrap & Co. in 1946. Joan Hassall was trained by Jackson at the evening classes in the Royal Academy Schools which she attended from 1928 to 1933.*
Jackson introduced her to the work of Bewick who became a major influence on her work.

Eliot Hodgkin (1905–1987)

80. *Asparagus*
tempera on panel
256:127 mm
signed and dated: *Eliot/Hodgkin/9 iv 75*
1976.23
Hodgkin studied under Jackson at both the RA Schools and at the Byam Shaw. Although teaching left Jackson little time to paint in tempera he encouraged his pupils to work in this exacting medium. According to Charles Stewart, Cennino Cennini's handbook, the essential source-book for tempera painters, was much in evidence in Jackson's painting classes.

Patrick Phillips (1907–1976)

81. *Head and shoulders of a female model*
graphite with two unrelated touches of green watercolour
145:90 mm (extended upper left and lower edge with strips of paper)
Lent from a private collection.
One of a number of studies submitted by the artist for the Prix de Rome while he was a student at the Byam Shaw School.

Charles Stewart (b.1915)

82. *Measured drawing of a rood-loft from Bois-le-Duc*
graphite with pen and black ink on smooth white paper laid down on panel
550:722 mm
inscribed in graphite below: *The principal elevation (West side)/ Roodloft from Bois-le-Duc; formerly in the Cathedral of St. John at Bois-le-Duc, North Brabant, and/ now in the Victoria and Albert Museum, London Measured and drawn by C. Stewart./ Scale of feet/ 1938*
Lent from a private collection.
The complex subject was set by Jackson as a exercise in precision drawing in the artist's last term at the Byam Shaw School. Begun in November 1937 it was completed the following February. Other students were allocated different subjects from the V. & A. This was not a standard exercise but was introduced in 1937 to extend the drawing range of the advanced students.

83. *Costume Study*
watercolour on wove paper
480:355 mm
A record of a costume of c.1889 formerly in the artist's possession and now in the museum of costume at Shambellie, Dumfriesshire.

84. *Costume Study*
graphite on wove paper
435: 295 mm
inscribed in graphite below: *Feb 3 1959 Rosie in brown satin dress c.1816/ Charles Stewart.*

Brian Dick Lauder Thomas (1912–1989)

85. *Head of a woman turned to left*
graphite on cream wove paper
265:200 mm
Presented by Dr J.G.P. Delaney 2000.7
Drawn in the "Jackson" manner by one of the most successful students of the Byam Shaw School. When the school reopened in 1946, Dick Thomas returned as joint Principal. He retired in 1954.

86. *The Angel of the Resurrection*
black chalk and bodycolour on stiff, buff paper
330:223 mm
Presented by Dr J.G.P. Delaney 2000.6
There is a larger study of the same composition in the Ashmolean, also elaborately coloured.

87. *Study for a stained glass window.*
graphite with grey and yellow wash touched with red and varnished on white paper
505:360 mm
Lent from a private collection.
Thomas was a distinguished stained-glass artist, best known for his work in St Paul's cathedral after the 1939–45 war. This is a drawing for a window in the O.B.E. chapel in St Paul's. He acquired a life-long affection for the Italian Renaissance while working under Jackson but extended this to include a particular interest in European Baroque art. The design and colour of this study derive from seventeenth-century stained glass.

Pamela Ovens (1903–1985)

88. *View on the Palatine*
oil on canvas
400:300 mm
Lent from a private collection.
Painted in November 1969. Pamela Ovens, who administered the Byam Shaw School while Jackson was Principal, was not his student in any formal sense but responded to the lessons nonetheless. She became director of the school when it reopened in 1946 and took up painting in earnest only after she had retired in 1962.

BIBLIOGRAPHY

A. Manuscript sources

Jackson's archives from the Byam Shaw School, including material from the earliest period of his career, were faithfully preserved by Pamela Ovens who, in turn, left them to Jackson's daughter, Mrs Betty Clark. She presented the bulk of the papers, including correspondence to and from Jackson, transcripts of his lectures, as well as tributes to him and correspondence about him and his work, to the Tate Gallery Archives.

Letters from Jackson to Mr and Mrs Joseph Pennell, Whistler-Pennell Collection, Box 234, Library of Congress, Washington,D.C.

B. Published sources

Anon, "Art at Brighton: Interesting Exhibition", *The Morning Post* (24 July 1922).
—, *Design and Industry: a Proposal for the Foundation of a Design and Industries Foundation* [c.1915].
—, "Studio Talk", *The Studio*, 18 (1900), pp.281-6.
Barman, Christian, *The Man who built London Transport: a Biography of Frank Pick*, Newton Abbott: David and Charles, 1979.
Brown, Bolton, *Lithography for Artists*, Scammon Lectures for the Art Institute of Chicago, 1929 [1930].
Delaney, J.G.P., *Charles Ricketts, a biography*, Oxford: Clarendon Press, 1990.
—, "Ernest Jackson, Draughtsman and Litho-grapher", *Apollo*, 125 (1987), pp. 338-43.
—, *Glyn Philpot, his Life and Art*, London: Ashgate Publishing, 1999.
—, "Peter Greenham, RA", *Apollo*, 125 (1987), pp.434-6.
Dodgson, Campbell and Pennell, Joseph, *The Senefelder Club*, London: XXI Gallery, Adelphi, 1922.
Dunstan, Bernard, The Paintings of Bernard Dunstan, London: David and Charles, 1993
Ellwood, G.M., "Famous Contemporary Art Masters III: F. E. Jackson", *Drawing and Design* (Feb 1924), pp. 758-65.
Harries, Meirion and Susie, *The War Artists*, London: Michael Joseph, 1983.

Hartrick, A. S., *Lithography as a fine art*, The Little Craft Books, ed. F. V. Burridge, Oxford: Oxford University Press, 1937.
—, *A Painter's Pilgrimage through Fifty Years*, Cambridge: Cambridge University Press, 1939.
Jackson, F. Ernest, "Lithography", *The Imprint*, 1 (17 Jan 1913), pp. XXX-X; (17 Feb 1913),pp. 125-7; (17 Mar 1913), pp.174-5.
—, "T. R. Way: Lithographer", *The Imprint*, 3 (17 Mar 1913), pp. 178-9.
—, "Modern Lithography", *Print Collector's Quarterly*, 11 (1925), pp. 205-26.
—, "The Artist and the Lithograph", *The Listener*, 1 (16 Jan 1929), p. 19; from a talk broadcast on Jan 10.
—, *Memorial Exhibition*, foreword by Lancelot Glasson, Beaux-Arts Gallery, Bruton Street, London 19 Nov - 16 Dec 1946.
—, *Notes from the Sketchbooks*, privately printed at the University Press, Oxford, 1947.
—, *Ernest Jackson, Drawings and Lithographs*, privately printed by the Byam Shaw School of Drawing and Painting Ltd [1955].
Nevinson, C.R.W., *Paint and Prejudice*, London: Methen, 1937.
Nicholson, C. A., "The Prints of Elsie Henderson", *Print Collector's Quarterly*, 15 (1928), pp. 315-37.
Pennell, Joseph, "The Senefelder Club and the Revival of Artistic Lithography", *The Studio*, 61 (Feb 1914), pp.3-5.
Radford, Ernest, "Mr Ernest Jackson's Lithographs", *The Studio*, 31, (1904), pp. 134-8.
Salaman, Malcolm, "The Great War: Britain's Efforts and Ideals Depicted by British Artists", *The Studio*, 71 (1917), pp. 103-27.
—, *Modern Woodcuts and Lithographs by British and French Artists*, London: The Studio, 1919.
—, *The Modern Colour-print of Original Design*, London: Broomhead, Cutts & Co., Ltd, 1920.
Singer, H. W., *Moderne Graphik*, Leipsig, 1920.
Slater, Frank, *Practical Portrait Drawing*, The New Art Library, 2 series, London nd.
Thomas, B.D.L., "Memorial Exhibition of the Paintings, Drawings and Lithographs of F. E. Jackson, A.R.A., at the Beaux-Arts Gallery", *Burlington Magazine*, 88 (Nov 1946), pp. 279-80.